Cocktails
and
Mixed Drinks

Cocktails and Mixed Drinks

Marilyn Harvey

This edition produced exclusively for

 WHSMITH

ACKNOWLEDGMENT

This work could not have been accomplished
without the cooperation and encouragement of
James McQuade, a Councillor of the United
Kingdom Bartenders Guild, who gave so readily
of his extensive knowledge of cocktails and mixed
drinks.

Cover photography by Michael Plomer

Line illustrations by Stewart Cowley

**This edition published exclusively for
W H Smith**

Published by
The Hamlyn Publishing Group Limited
London · New York · Sydney · Toronto
Astronaut House, Feltham, Middlesex, England
Copyright © The Hamlyn Publishing Group Limited 1982
Reprinted 1983
Third impression 1983
ISBN 0 600 37888 8

Printed in Italy

Contents

Introduction

The cocktail is a relative newcomer to the world of alcoholic beverages. Crude pottery wine jars dating back thousands of years B.C. have been found in Greece and Asia Minor and virtually every civilization since has left a record of some association with wine or beer.

Alcohol is a product of a reaction which occurs naturally and which is known as fermentation. The atmosphere contains wild yeasts which have an affinity for sugar. Once these yeasts come in contact with sugar they begin devouring it, breaking it down into its constituent parts until all that remains is water and alcohol. When these yeasts settle on a bunch of ripe grapes they set to work on the juicy sugary liquid and within a few days the juice has fermented to wine. Much the same occurs with wet grain and yeasts, so producing beer. Mankind has improved on this process over the centuries, but both wine and beer are essentially nature's products.

Not so with spirits. It is not known whether the art of distillation was invented in the Middle or Far East, but it was the Arabs who perfected the technique in their quest for perfumes and they gave us the word, 'alcohol'. In the distillation process the wine, beer or other fermented liquid is heated to a temperature that causes the alcohol content to evaporate, but as this temperature is lower than the boiling point of water, the water content remains in the still. The alcoholic vapours are collected and cooled, so that the resulting liquid is almost pure alcohol. This is then diluted with distilled water and sold as spirit. Much of the character of the original ingredients is carried over into the spirit which is why gin, whisky, tequila, vodka and rum all have different aromas and flavours.

Liqueurs were the first alcoholic beverages to be distilled for drinking purposes. Doctors and herbalists prescribed the 'essences' because of the medicinal properties of the original ingredients. In medieval times religious orders were the main source of medical knowledge and, consequently, the treatment of physical disorders with distilled essences of herbs meant that monks became associated with liqueurs. The recipe for Chartreuse, for example, has been with the brothers at the Monastery of La Grande Chartreuse in France since 1605 and is still made today at the monastery to the same recipe, which is known to contain over 130 herbs and spices. France, Italy and Holland are the three main liqueur-producing countries but there are thousands of liqueurs throughout the world, many of them known only in their local area of production. One liqueur that was a local favourite in Saronno, Italy, in the 16th century was once given as a thank-you present to an artist. He was painting the now-famous religious frescos in the local

sanctuary and used the young widow who ran the village inn as his model for the Madonna. In return she distilled some fresh apricots and their kernels into a drink for him – today Amaretto di Saronno is a liqueur of international repute.

It was not until the early 19th century that spirits and liqueurs were being mixed together to create new drinks. There are dozens of explanations as to the origin of the word, 'cocktail'. One of the most likely is that it is an Americanization of the French, *'coquetel'*, which was a mixed wine drink taken to America by Lafayette's soldiers when France supported the colonies in their revolution against Britain. Mixed drinks were not known widely until the first cocktail era in the Roaring Twenties. At this time cocktails were short drinks such as the Bronx, Clover Club, Sidecar and White Lady, all popular with the fashionable sets of 'Bright Young Things' in London, Paris and New York.

Prohibition had the ironic effect of increasing interest in mixed drinks. The scarcity of reputably made liquor led to the prevalence of moonshine and bath-tub concoctions which needed to be mixed with something else to make them palatable. Heavily flavoured bitters, fruit syrups and juices were used in abundance, so that once Prohibition was lifted, the American populace had developed a taste for mixed drinks.

The American GI carried this preference with him, so that postwar Europe was educated to the idea as well.

The late Seventies saw another cocktail boom with the accent on long drinks such as the Harvey Wallbanger and Tequila Sunrise, and the blender has opened another horizon to cocktail lovers with its frozen fruit Daiquiris, Pina Coladas and ice-cream drinks. Today the cocktail is no longer an exotic speciality but a refreshing flavoursome drink available to all.

Useful Facts and Figures

Miscellaneous

dash = 5 drops
teaspoon = $\frac{1}{8}$ fl oz
dessertspoon = $\frac{1}{4}$ fl oz
tablespoon = $\frac{1}{2}$ fl oz
6-out measure = $\frac{5}{6}$ fl oz
5-out measure = 1 fl oz
4-out measure = $1\frac{1}{4}$ fl oz
pong (U.S.A.) = 1 fl oz (approx.)
jigger (U.S.A.) = $1\frac{1}{2}$ fl oz (approx.)
Cocktail glasses vary from 2 to $3\frac{1}{2}$ oz.
$2\frac{1}{2}$ oz is an average U.K. size

4-oz wine glass (U.S.A.); a good size
for sours, like vodka and tomato juice.
A U.K. size is a 5-oz wine glass.
14·2 cl = 5 fl oz = 1 gill or noggin

23 cl = U.K. 8-oz wine glass

28·4 cl = 10 fl oz = U.K. half-pint.
Tumblers can be smaller, but 10 oz
gives wider scope
33 cl = 12-oz wine glass
56 cl = U.K. pint
75 cl = One 'reputed' quart = usual
wine bottle
100 cl = 1 litre

Measures and glasses – equivalent capacities

Centilitres (cl)	U.K. fluid ounces (fl oz)	U.S.A. liquid or fluid ounces (lq oz)
0·1	0·03	0·03
0·5	0·18	0·17
1	0·35	0·34
2	0·70	0·68
3	1·06	1·01
4	1·40	1·35
5	1·76	1·69
6	2·11	2·03
7	2·46	2·37
8	2·82	2·71
9	3·17	3·04
10	3·52	3·38
11	3·87	3·72
12	4·22	4·06
13	4·58	4·40
14	4·93	4·73
15	5·28	5·07
16	5·63	5·41
17	5·98	5·75
18	6·34	6·09
19	6·69	6·42
20	7·04	6·77
21	7·39	7·10
22	7·74	7·44
23	8·10	7·78
24	8·45	8·12
25	8·80	8·45
26	9·15	8·80
27	9·50	9·13
28	9·85	9·47
29	10·21	9·81
30	10·56	10·14
50	17·60	16·91
75	26·40	25·36
100	35·20	33·81

1·14 litres = 40 fl oz = 8·0 gills =
One Imperial quart = ¼ Imperial gallon.

Comparison of small measures

U.K.

---

1 gill or noggin = 14·2 cl
6-out (of a gill) = 2·37 cl
5-out (of a gill) = 2·84 cl
4-out (of a gill) = 3·55 cl
2-out (of a gill) = 7·10 cl

4 gills = 1 Imperial pint = 20 fl oz =
   56·8 cl
2 pints = 1 Imperial quart = 40 fl oz =
   113·6 cl (U.K. large spirit bottle)
4 quarts = 1 Imperial gallon =
   160 fl oz = 4·55 litres = 277·42 cubic
   inches

U.S.A.

---

pong = 1 lq oz (approx.) = 2·96 cl
jigger = $1\frac{1}{2}$ lq oz (approx.) = 4·44 cl
pint = 16 lq oz = 47·32 cl
quart = 32 lq oz = 94·64 cl
4 quarts = 1 U.S. gallon = 128 lq oz
   = 3·784 litres (0·833 Imperial
   gallons) = 231 cubic inches

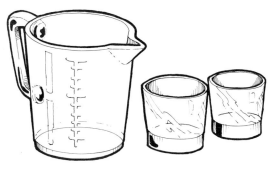

Conversion table

To change from	to	multiply by
grams	ounces	0·035
ounces	grams	28·35
kilograms	pounds	2·205
pounds	kilograms	0·454
centilitres	fluid ounces (U.K.)	0·352
centilitres	liquid ounces (U.S.A.)	0·338
gallons (U.K.)	litres	4·50
gallons (U.S.A.)	litres	3·80
litres	centilitres	10·00

Temperatures
°F to °C deduct 32 and multiply by 5/9
°C to °F multiply by 9/5 and add 32

Anatomy of a Cocktail

A cocktail is created by combining a number of ingredients. Each consituent has its own flavour, but when mixed together the resulting drink takes on a character of its own. It is essential that the flavour of no single ingredient should dominate a cocktail as the intention is to create an entirely new taste. The ingredients of a cocktail fall into three main categories.

Base Usually the basic constituent of a cocktail is a spirit. This determines the style of drink it is, so that if it contains gin, it becomes a gin-based cocktail. Most of the cocktails that have been successful for many years have at least 50% of the base spirit. Examples of this are the White Lady, the Manhattan, the Daiquiri and the Sidecar. Some recipes, such as the Between-the-Sheets, are able to combine two base spirits successfully, but drinks containing three or more spirits are rarely well-balanced as the flavours and aromas compete with each other rather than marry together.

Modifier Each cocktail has an ingredient that modifies the character of the base spirit so that the combination of the base and the modifier creates a new flavour sensation. It is essential to add the correct proportion of the modifying ingredient to achieve the desired effect. A recipe that states five parts gin and one part dry vermouth requires the gin to be 5/6 of the drink and the vermouth 1/6 of it – any variation from these proportions will produce a drink with a different character, as any Martini lover is prepared to explain at some length! Liqueurs, aromatic beverages such as vermouths, dairy products and fruit juices are the most widely used modifiers.

Special additives Many cocktails contain ingredients that contribute to the flavour or colour of the drinks. Gomme syrup features in numerous cocktails as the sweetening agent and non-alcoholic fruit syrups can provide both colour and flavour. For example, grenadine is vital in a Pink Lady. Often the sweetness of a liqueur or syrup equalizes the acidity of citrus juices. Angostura bitters are an integral part of many cocktails as they heighten the flavour of some combinations of ingredients which might otherwise be too bland together, such as in the Rob Roy or Champagne Cocktail. Several recipes require an ingredient to be splashed over the top of the drink either to add extra character or colour effect. The Galliano in a Harvey Wallbanger and the Campari in a Pink Grapefruit are added for these reasons. Egg white and cream are used as special additives because of the effect they have on the texture of drinks as is obvious in a Whisky Sour or Grasshopper. Also it is important to realize that the modifier in one drink may be the special additive in another, so take note of quantities. Ingredients that are special additives are meant to be used sparingly and recipes usually indicate that only dashes are needed. Over-enthusiasm when adding these ingredients can seriously upset the balance of taste, texture or colour of a drink.

PRESENTATION

A drink must be correctly presented before it can properly be described as a cocktail, although, during Prohibition in the U.S.A., Martinis were drunk from many a teacup with not an olive in sight. There are some recipes where the garnish has an effect on the flavour of the drink. This is

particularly true where citrus rind is used as the essential oils contained in the skin add aroma and flavour to the cocktail. A Moscow Mule has half a lime squeezed into the drink, then the spent shell is dropped in as well to strengthen the 'zing' as well as give visual appeal.

There is something very inviting about a beautifully presented cocktail. A delightful sense of anticipation is aroused which in turn stimulates a feeling of thirst. Many a person has decided not to bother with a drink until he sees a glistening cold glass brimming with a colourful concoction. The secret of a successful cocktail is its attractive appearance as this excites the appetite and awakens the taste buds which begin limbering up for the first sip.

Equipment

There are a few specialized items needed for cocktail mixing but generally most households already have much of the equipment in the kitchen. It is a good idea when setting up a cocktail bar or cabinet to stock it with most of the equipment as it is time consuming and aggravating to have to search around the kitchen for several different items just to make a simple cocktail before dinner or when guests arrive unexpectedly. Cocktail equipment must be rinsed thoroughly after use. Liqueurs will leave it sticky and acidic juices will erode silver plate. Also, many ingredients used in cocktail mixing have pungent aromas which will linger and contaminate other drinks made in the same equipment unless it is kept scrupulously clean.

Shaker The best shaker for home use is the three-piece one in stainless steel as it has a built-in strainer. The one-pint shaker will hold enough liquid to make three short drinks comfortably. The first purpose of the shaker is to mix ingredients thoroughly, especially in those recipes containing juices, eggs, creams and syrups. The second purpose is to chill the drink properly. The shaker should be filled three quarters full of ice and the drink then strained off the ice unless the recipe specifies otherwise.

Mixing glass This is actually a glass with a pouring lip which holds over a pint of liquid. Ingredients that do not need to be shaken together to amalgamate are stirred through ice in a mixing glass to chill them thoroughly. The drink is always strained from a mixing glass and if one is not available the base of a shaker will serve the same purpose.

Barspoon The spoon is ten inches long with a teaspoon at one end and a flat metal disc at the other. The disc is known as the muddler and is used to crush sugar and other ingredients together in recipes such as the Mint Julep and Old-Fashioned. The metal shaft of the spoon is twisted so that when it is rubbed backwards and forwards between the hands, the spoon mixes the ingredients through the ice with a twisting action.

Corkscrew There is a variety of shapes and sizes available. The professional bartender uses a shape known as the 'waiters' friend' which has a bottle opener at one end and a small knife and corkscrew at the other.

Strainer A bar strainer (Hawthorn-type) is a flat disc with a short handle, there are holes in the disc and a coiled spring surrounds it. When the strainer is put into the mixing glass or shaker the spring fits itself to the utensil and holds back the ice. Blended drinks that require straining need a bar strainer which has two metal lugs that can rest on the edge of the blender.

Ice crusher There are manual and electric ice crushers. It is possible to crush ice cubes by putting them in a towel and hitting them with a wooden kitchen hammer.

Electric blender Most family kitchens are equipped with a blender that is quite suitable for making drinks. Take care to use crushed ice and blend on a slow speed or the blades will suffer too much wear.

Straws Plastic straws have the strength necessary to cope with immersion in long drinks. Drinks with a milkshake texture, such as drinks made in a blender, need thick straws and frappés are best served with short straws.

Stirrers It is possible to collect stirrers from most cocktail bars. They are necessary accessories for many long drinks and make interesting conversation pieces.

Coasters Coasters are needed to protect the table surface from scratches and watermarks.

Napkins Iced drinks often leave guests with wet hands and many cocktails can be quite sticky if they are spilt. It is very thoughtful for the host or hostess to place a napkin nearby in case it is needed quickly.

Ice bucket A well-balanced and well-insulated ice bucket will keep ice cubes for a few hours. A metal or plastic scoop is needed so that the ice is not handled in front of guests.

Water jug A small water jug is useful for those drinks requiring water.

Glassware

Inviting presentation is essential with mixed drinks and a cocktail served in the style of glass most suitable to the drink looks especially attractive. Clear glassware enhances the colours of the drink and its garnish, and good quality glass will highlight the effort and care the host or hostess has taken to present the guest with a delicious drink. A clear fine-rimmed glass with a stable base is ideal for cocktails.

Glassware should be stored out of reach of children and polished with a clean dry cloth prior to use to give it that extra sparkle. Offering the cocktail from a tray enables the guest to appreciate the full effect of the prepared drink and care must be taken to ensure that the glass is not too full of liquid or an accident is likely. The following are the main styles of glassware.

Balloon The balloon-shaped glass has a short stem and is designed specifically for brandy. The intention is that the bowl can be held between two hands so that body heat warms the drink, thereby releasing extra aroma. The French prefer to drink brandy from a style of glass similar to a sherry glass.

Cocktail glass The stemmed cocktail glass has a capacity of 3–4 oz/75–100 ml and the bowl may be rounded or straight sided. This is the traditional size for short drinks.

Double cocktail glass This has a capacity of 6–7 oz/175–200 ml. It is suitable for frappés and is being used increasingly for strained blended drinks and ice-cream drinks.

Flute The flute has an elongated bowl with straight sides and often has a long stem as well. This elegant glass is used for champagne and sparkling wine drinks. The long narrow bowl allows the bubbles to come to the surface in a continuous stream.

Goblet The stemmed glass known as a Paris goblet holds about 6–12 oz/175–350 ml and is a good all-purpose glass suitable for many mixed drinks, hot drinks and beer.

Highball The straight-sided highball glass has a capacity of 8–12 oz/225–350 ml and is used for long drinks and beer.

Hot drink glass This glass stands on a short stem and has a handle. Made of heat-resistant glass, it is ideal for speciality coffees and hot mixed drinks.

Liqueur glass The small-stemmed liqueur glass holds $1-2\frac{1}{2}$ oz/25–60 ml and is also used for 'one-shot' servings of ice-cold schnapps and aquavit (or akvavit).

Sherry Glass The sherry glass has an elongated bowl on a stem. It has a capacity of 4 oz/100 ml and may be used for sherry, port and madeira.

Tulip This glass is so named because of the shape of the bowl. It is ideal for red wine as the slight narrowing at the top allows the aroma to gather in the bowl.

Old fashioned This short straight-sided tumbler is used for spirit drinks that are served over ice.

Ingredients

Bitters These beverages are so called because they are bitter tasting and are meant to have digestive or medical properties. Those most widely used in cocktail mixing are Angostura bitters, Fernet Branca, Campari and orange bitters. Most recipes indicate that bitters be used in small quantities as they are very strongly flavoured.

Coconut cream Most good supermarkets now carry coconut cream in cans. It has a very concentrated flavour and only a little is necessary to provide a drink with a delicious coconut flavour and creamy texture. Too much coconut cream leaves a greasy ring on the glass and the drink is very sickly.* Creamed coconut which comes in packets and coconut oil are not substitutes as the former is used for curries and the latter for cookery purposes.

Consommé Cans of consommé can be kept for Bullshots, Bloodshots and Hot Shots.

Cream Fresh cream creates a drink with a velvety texture. It is important not to use too much of it as cream can mask the flavours of the other ingredients. Cream can be used to highlight the presentation of a drink by floating it on the liquid. Place a spoon in the glass with the back upturned and slowly pour the cream over the back of the spoon. This will allow it to settle on

---

* *Coconut cream will separate after standing for a long period. Blend the entire contents of an opened can for a few seconds to return it to its creamy consistency. It can be kept refrigerated in an airtight container for about two weeks.*

top of the drink. Both the White Russian and Irish Coffee have cream on top.

Egg white This is a most useful additive to many cocktails as it adds body and interest to the presentation of a drink. When mixing cocktails put two egg whites in a small jug and cut through them a few times to separate them properly. Then a dash can be poured into a shaker whenever required.

Gomme syrup This is ready-made sugar syrup and is available by the bottle in most outlets that sell liquor. Most mixed drinks need a little sweetening to balance the flavour and because ordinary crystals of sugar would leave a gritty taste, gomme syrup is recommended. It is possible to make sugar syrup at home by slowly dissolving 3 cups of sugar in 1 cup of water. Boil the dissolved mixture for a few minutes. When cool it may be kept indefinitely.

Grenadine This is a non-alcoholic fruit syrup made from pomegranates. It has a bright red colour which is most useful in mixing cocktails. It is sold by most liquor stores. Other flavours of syrups are commercially available, e.g. fraise (strawberry), framboise (raspberry), orgeat (almond), and cassis (blackcurrant).

Ice Abundant supplies of ice cubes and crushed ice can be stored in the freezer in plastic containers. This way the ice has had time to refreeze properly after being removed from the cube trays. Ice that is on the point of melting is of little use in cocktails as it cannot chill the drink properly.

Ice-cream Ice-cream with a good creamy texture makes excellent cocktails. The soft ice-cream, often sold by speciality shops or ice-cream vans, is ideal.

Juices Fresh orange, grapefruit and pineapple juices are available in cartons and they will last in the refrigerator for about three days. Lemon and lime juices are best squeezed fresh for each cocktail-mixing session as the extra piquancy of the fresh juices makes them preferable. Cans of tomato juice are a good standby for Bloody Marys and a good quality lime-juice cordial is a useful addition to the store cupboard.

Minerals Bottles of tonic, dry ginger ale, cola, carbonated lemonade or 7-Up and soda water can be kept for some months in a dark cool place. Alternatively, a mineral maker is a good invest-ment for those who entertain frequently or households with thirsty children.

Spices Worcestershire and Tabasco sauces are needed for a number of mixed drinks.

Garnishing

It is vital that a cocktail be properly presented if it is to have visual appeal, as the adage, 'man eats with his eyes,' applies even more so to drinking. Garnishing should be simple but elegant and must add something positive to the presentation. A cocktail that is over decorated is not only unattractive but difficult as it is necessary to fight through the jungle of decoration to reach the drink.

Celery The top of the celery stalk is tender and juicy. Prepare it so that some foliage still remains on the stalk as it looks very inviting to serve a Bloody Mary with the greenery above the red colour of the drink. The celery can be used as a stirrer and is edible.

Cherries The most attractive cherries are those which still have stalks on them as they look elegant in a cocktail glass. They are available in bottles from high-class delicatessens. Red Maraschino cherries are the most popular.

Citrus fruits Limes, lemons and oranges are frequently used for garnishing as they add flavour to the drink as well as provide colour to the presentation. Citrus fruits are prepared in the following ways.

Slice Evenly cut slices about 1/8 inch/3 mm thick can be used either in whole 'cartwheel' fashion or half-section.

Spent shell The remains of the half shell after it has been squeezed into the drink can be attractive.

Wedge Cut an eighth section of the fruit lengthwise. Nick the wedge across the pulp and squeeze it before dropping it into the drink.

Zest This is a small thin piece of the peel without the pith. It should be squeezed over the drink before dropping it in, as this releases essential oils.

Twist This is a longer piece of citrus peel which can be twisted in the centre.

Spiral The complete peel of the fruit is arranged in the glass in spiral fashion, with one end over the lip of the glass. This garnish is *de rigueur* for a Horse's Neck and the Country Club Cooler.

Cucumber A strip of skin from a cucumber can be cut lengthwise, so that it stands the full length of a highball glass. This green strip looks particularly refreshing and is the classic garnish for a Pimms.

Mint Fresh mint has a very high oil content which emits a strong minty aroma which complements many long drinks. It is an essential ingredient for the Mint Julep and looks attractive in punches and cups. Make sure it is well washed and use only young tender parts.

Olives Small juicy green olives are best used in clear drinks served in a cocktail glass.

Pineapple Drinks containing pineapple juice are sometimes garnished with wedges of fresh pineapple. Cut a slice from the unpeeled fruit, ½ inch/13 mm thick, then cut it into eighths. Cut a small nick into the wedge and insert this over the rim of the glass.

Spices Cinnamon, nutmeg and coffee can be dusted over hot drinks or creamy mixtures. The Alexander and the Nassau Express look very attractive with a fine dusting on top.

Strawberries A small ripe red strawberry, complete with its green stalk, makes a pretty garnish if it is slit halfway through and inserted over the edge of a glass. This is particularly suitable for the Strawberry Daiquiri and Strawberry Dawn.

Sugar The rim of a glass can be frosted with sugar by running a cut wedge of lemon around the edge to moisten it, then inverting the glass into a saucer of finely granulated white sugar. This is the classic decoration for a Brandy Crusta.

Explanatory Terms and Symbols

Below is a guide to some of the terms used throughout this book and beside them are some symbols which may prove useful.

Serve chilled

This term is used throughout the book when a recipe requires stirring. Three-quarters fill the mixing glass with ice, then add ingredients. Introduce the barspoon to the mixture and stir in a circular fashion, twisting the shaft of the spoon between your fingers. Another method is to rub the spoon shaft vigorously between both hands until the mixture is sufficiently chilled. When ready, use a Hawthorn-type bar-strainer (*see* page 21) to hold back the ice while the drink is poured.

Shake

Three-quarters fill the shaker with ice, then add ingredients. Secure the top to the base and grasp firmly with both hands making sure that there is no chance of it accidentally coming apart while shaking. Shake vigorously for a few seconds using both hands until frost appears on the outside of the receptacle. Strain as quickly as possible after the operation is complete into the required glass.

Blend

Put required amount of ice into the jug of the blender, then add the ingredients. Regulate the speed according to how much ice is used. The more ice, the slower it should be regulated so that the correct texture will be achieved. Also, the more fresh fruit, e.g. bananas, strawberries and peaches, added, the more time will be required for the blender to run. Recipes containing only ice-cream and liquid should be blended on a fast speed for only a few seconds. The maximum time for the blender to run should not exceed 30 seconds as damage may occur to the motor.

Prepare in Glass Some recipes are made by pouring the ingredients straight into the glass in which they are drunk. Usually, but not always, the drink requires ice and therefore the glass should be stirred as each ingredient is added.

Before-Dinner Drinks

Everyday living in this modern world usually means moving at a frenetic pace. We rush to work, hustle and bustle all day, and are swept home on a tide of peak-hour traffic. Often there's the super-market shopping to do, the dash to pick up the children and 101 tiny crises to overcome, while the clock keeps us scurrying along through the daily routine.

The evening meal is often regarded as just another necessity that has its appointed time and, as such, is usually dispensed with quickly. However, many people are now reverting to one of the more gracious habits of the prewar world, the aperitif before the evening meal. The simple act of having a drink before dinner creates time for conversation between people who probably have not seen each other since early morning and the pause allows recovery from the day's events. This, in turn, makes mealtime more pleasurable.

The early evening is treasured in many parts of the world as time for relaxation. The French sit for hours in their cafés, sipping pastis drinks and, in the long autumn evenings, the men play boules in the park, the women chat and everyone drinks kir before strolling home for dinner. The Italian piazzas are lined with tables and chairs to accommodate the office workers who arrive for their vermouth. The pre-dinner drink is so much a part of life in the U.S.A. that the early evening has long been called the cocktail hour.

A drink that is served as an aperitif is meant to

sharpen the appetite and prepare the diner for the meal. Furthermore, many drinks actually aid digestion. Sugar depresses the desire for food so cocktails with cream or a high liqueur content are best kept for after dinner. The best-known pre-dinner cocktails are short drinks with a sharp taste. Many of them are quite alcoholic as they are meant to be drunk slowly. Recipes often include lime or lemon to provide the tang that starts the gastric juices flowing.

Gin is the spirit most associated with pre-dinner cocktails because of its affinity to citrus fruits. The juniper berry is the main flavouring agent of gin and contributes the distinctive aroma to the spirit. Vermouth drinks are also suitable as aperitifs because the bitter flavour sharpens the appetite and marries well with spirit. This characteristic bitterness comes from the herbs, spices and plant roots that are macerated in wine to produce vermouth. The classic combination of gin and vermouth is called the Martini.

Many of these drinks are quickly and easily prepared, using ingredients kept in most households. Try a Bullshot before lunch or a sour before dinner to understand why the aperitif is returning to fashion. It is a valuable aid to relaxation.

Americano
1 part Campari
1 part sweet vermouth
soda water
Stir the Campari and sweet vermouth into an ice-filled goblet or whisky glass. Add the soda and a slice of orange.

Antoine's Smile
3 parts calvados
1 part lemon juice
1 part gomme gyrup
1 dash grenadine
Shake.

Appetizer
1 part vodka
1 part Mandarine Napoléon
1 part fresh lime juice
1 dash egg white
Shake.

Apricot Sour
1 part apricot brandy
1 part lemon juice
1 dash Angostura bitters
1 dash egg white
wedge of apricot
Shake the first four ingredients together. Decorate with a wedge of apricot.

Balalaika
1 part vodka
1 part Cointreau
1 part lemon juice
Shake.

36

Blue Lagoon

1 part vodka
1 part blue curaçao
carbonated lemonade or 7-Up

Stir the vodka and the blue curaçao into an ice-filled highball glass. Top with carbonated lemonade or 7-Up.

Bobby Burns

1 part Scotch whisky
1 part sweet vermouth
3 dashes Benedictine

Serve chilled.

Bronx

3 parts gin
1 part dry vermouth
1 part sweet vermouth
1 part orange juice

Shake.

Bullshot

1 part vodka
4 parts beef consommé
1 dash lemon juice
2 dashes Worcestershire sauce
1 pinch celery salt

Shake. Strain into a large glass.

Cardinale

3 dashes crème de cassis
dry red wine

Add the wine to the cassis in a wine goblet.

Champagne Cocktail

1 cube sugar
3 dashes Angostura bitters
1 dash brandy
champagne

Place the cube of sugar in a tulip or flute glass. Add the Angostura bitters and the brandy and top with chilled champagne. Add a slice of orange and a cherry.

37

Clover Club
6 parts gin
2 parts grenadine
1 part lemon juice
1 dash egg white
Shake. Strain into a wine goblet.

Daiquiri
3 parts white rum
1 part fresh lime juice
3 dashes gomme syrup
Shake.

Dry Martini
5 parts gin
1 part dry vermouth
Serve chilled or on the rocks. Add a twist of lemon.

Dubonnet Cocktail
1 part gin
1 part Dubonnet
Serve chilled. Add a twist of lemon.

Fino Mac
2 parts dry sherry
1 part ginger wine
Serve chilled.

Fraise Royale
2 fresh strawberries
2 dashes fraise liqueur
2 dashes chilled champagne
Blend together and pour into a tulip or a flute glass. Top with additional chilled champagne.

Gimlet
2 parts gin
1 part lime juice cordial
Serve on the rocks. Add a splash of soda if required.

Gin and It
1 part gin
1 part sweet vermouth
Serve gin and sweet vermouth straight into a
cocktail glass. Add a cherry.

Gin Fizz
2 parts gin
1 part lemon juice
2 dashes gomme syrup
soda water
Shake the gin, lemon juice and gomme syrup and
strain into a goblet. Top with soda water.

Kir
Dry white wine
3 dashes crème de cassis
Put crème de cassis in a wine goblet and top with
dry white wine.

Macaroni
2 parts pastis
1 part sweet vermouth
Serve chilled.

Maiden's Prayer
3 parts gin
3 parts Cointreau
1 part orange juice
1 part lemon juice
Shake.

Mandarine Sour
1 part Mandarine Napoléon
1 part lemon juice
2 dashes Angostura bitters
1 dash egg white
Shake and strain into a wine glass. Add a slice of
orange.

Manhattan
2 parts rye whisky
1 part sweet vermouth
1 dash Angostura bitters
Serve chilled or on the rocks and decorate with a cherry.

Negroni
1 part gin
1 part sweet vermouth
1 part Campari
soda water
Mix gin, sweet vermouth and Campari in an ice-filled old-fashioned glass. Soda is optional. Add a slice of orange.

Orange Blossom
1 part gin
1 part orange juice
Shake.

Perfect Lady
2 parts gin
1 part peach brandy
1 part lemon juice
1 dash egg white
Shake.

Ramos Fizz
2 parts gin
2 parts lemon juice
1 dash gomme syrup
3 dashes orange flower water
3 dashes cream
1 egg white
soda water
Shake all the ingredients except the soda water and strain into a large goblet. Top with soda.

Rob Roy

1 part Scotch whisky
1 part sweet vermouth
1 dash Angostura bitters
Serve chilled. A cherry is added as a garnish when the other ingredients have been poured into the cocktail glass.

Sakini

3 parts gin
1 part sake
Serve chilled or on the rocks.

Sazerac

1 large measure rye whisky
2 dashes Angostura bitters
3 drops pastis
2 dashes gomme syrup
Serve chilled or on the rocks. Add a twist of lemon peel.

Silent Third

1 part Scotch whisky
1 part Cointreau
1 part lemon juice
Shake.

Strawberry Martini

3 parts gin
1 part Chambéryzette
Serve chilled.

Suissesse

1 part pastis
1 part lemon juice
1 egg white
soda water
Shake pastis, lemon juice and egg white together and strain into a small wine glass. Splash in some soda.

S.W.1.
1 part vodka
1 part Campari
1 part orange juice
1 dash egg white
Shake.

Vodkatini
5 parts vodka
1 part dry vermouth
Serve chilled or on the rocks. Add a twist of lemon.

Whisky Sour
1 part whisky
1 part lemon juice
2 dashes gomme syrup
1 dash egg white
Shake. Add a slice of lemon.

White Lady
2 parts gin
1 part Cointreau
1 part lemon juice
1 dash egg white
Shake.

X.Y.Z.
2 parts rum
1 part Cointreau
1 part lemon juice
Shake.

After-Dinner Drinks

It is a well-established custom to offer guests a drink after dinner. It is an even better idea to enjoy the comforts of home by relaxing with some quiet music and a drink, when just the two of you are together once dinner is over and the children are in bed.

The French describe drinks served after dinner as '*digestifs*' because they aid digestion. It is quite extraordinary how quickly the effects of over-indulgence at the dinner table can pass, with the help of a glass of cognac! The fine bouquet, palate-cleansing taste and warming finish of a good brandy make it one of the most universally popular post-prandial drinks. Brandies made from fruits are known as Eaux-de-vie and include Kirsch (cherries), Poire Williams (pears), Calvados (apples), Mirabelle (plums), and Framboise (raspberries). These spirits have a haunting taste and a small glass of Eau-de-vie, served ice cold, is an unusual finish to a special dinner.

Liqueurs have a high sugar content which makes them very suitable for serving after dinner. Each liqueur has its own distinctive flavour and is a versatile mixer. Many cocktails contain at least one liqueur. Cream is an ingredient of some of the most popular after-dinner cocktails as it imparts a velvety texture to a drink. The combination of a liqueur and cream creates an attractive flavoursome drink that appeals particularly to women.

The frappé is one of the most delightful ways to

enjoy a liqueur after dinner. The liqueur is poured over finely crushed ice in a long-stemmed glass and sipped slowly through a short straw so that the full character of the liqueur can be appreciated. Crème de menthe is often served this way as an afternoon refreshment in hot countries. Kummel also makes an excellent after-dinner frappé as the caraway seeds from which it is made have been recognized as an aid to digestion for many centuries.

After Eight
1 part Scotch whisky
1 part Royal Mint Chocolate liqueur
1 part cream
chocolate for grating
Shake the whisky, liqueur and cream together and pour into a cocktail glass. Grate chocolate on top.

Alexander
1 part brandy
1 part brown crème de cacao
1 part cream
Shake. Sprinkle nutmeg on top.

44

Bacardi
3 parts Bacardi rum
1 part lemon or lime juice
2 dashes grenadine
Shake.

Banana Bliss
1 part brandy
1 part banana liqueur
Serve chilled.

Barbara
2 parts vodka
1 part brown crème de cacao
1 part cream
Shake.

B & B
1 part brandy
1 part Benedictine
Serve straight into a liqueur glass.

Between-the-Sheets
1 part brandy
1 part white rum
1 part Cointreau
1 dash lemon juice
Shake.

Black Russian
2 parts vodka
1 part Kahlua
Serve on the rocks.

Bosom Caresser
2 parts brandy
1 part orange curaçao
1 egg yolk
2 dashes grenadine
Shake. Serve in a double cocktail glass.

Brandy Crusta

2 parts brandy
1 part orange curaçao
1 dash Angostura bitters
3 dashes maraschino
1 dash lemon juice

Shake. Strain into an ice-filled sugar-rimmed goblet. Add a large twist of orange and a cherry.

Brave Bull

1 part tequila
1 part Kahlua

Stir into an ice-filled old-fashioned glass.

Coconut Daiquiri

2 parts coconut liqueur
2 parts fresh lime juice
1 part white rum
1 dash egg white

Shake.

Fifth Avenue

1 part brown crème de cacao
1 part apricot brandy
1 part cream

Pour carefully in order given into a straight-sided liqueur glass so that each ingredient floats on the preceding one.

French 75

1 part gin
1 part lemon juice
2 dashes gomme syrup
chilled champagne

Shake the gin, lemon juice and gomme syrup together. Serve, unstrained with ice, into a high-ball glass. Top with chilled champagne.

Golden Cadillac
1 part Galliano
1 part white crème de cacao
1 part cream
Shake.

Golden Dream
1 part Galliano
1 part Cointreau
1 part orange juice
1 part cream
Shake.

Golden Glow
1 part Galliano
1 part Drambuie
1 part gin
Serve chilled.

Golden Medallion
1 part Galliano
1 part cognac
1 part orange juice
1 dash egg white
Shake. Add zest of orange.

Grasshopper
1 part white crème de cacao
1 part green crème de menthe
1 part cream
Shake.

Mint Royal
1 part brandy
1 part Royal Mint Chocolate liqueur
1 part lemon juice
1 dash egg white
Shake.

47

Paradise

2 parts gin
1 part apricot brandy
1 part orange juice
Shake.

Pink Camelia

3 parts gin
2 parts apricot brandy
2 parts orange juice
2 parts lemon juice
1 part Campari
1 dash egg white
Shake.

Pink Lady

4 parts gin
1 part grenadine
1 part cream
2 dashes egg white
Shake.

Rolls Royce

1 part brandy
1 part Cointreau
1 part orange juice
Shake.

Scotch Frog

2 parts vodka
1 part Galliano
1 part Cointreau
juice of 1 lime
1 dash Angostura bitters
2 dashes maraschino cherry juice
Shake.

48

Sidecar

2 parts brandy
1 part Cointreau
1 part lemon juice
Shake.

Silk Stockings

3 parts tequila
2 parts white crème de cacao
3 parts cream
1 dash grenadine
1 scoop of crushed ice
Blend. Serve in a tulip glass and sprinkle cinnamon on the top. Serve with straws.

Velvet Hammer

1 part Cointreau
1 part Tia Maria
1 part cream
Shake.

White Russian

2 parts vodka
1 part Kahlua
cream
Mix the vodka and Kahlua in an ice-filled old-fashioned glass. Float the cream on top.

Yellow Bird

3 parts white rum
1 part Galliano
1 part Cointreau
1 part fresh lime juice
Shake with cracked ice and pour, unstrained, into a goblet. Add a slice of lime if available.

49

USING LIQUEURS

Liqueur	Flavour	Recipes
Advocaat	eggs and brandy	Easter Eggs, Fluffy Duck, Snowball.
Amaretto	almond	French Connection, Godfather, Godmother, Quiet Sunday, Sicilian Kiss.
Apricot Brandy	apricot	Apricot Sour, Fifth Avenue, Frozen Apricot Sour, Paradise, Pink Camelia, Zombie.
Benedictine	aromatic herbs	B & B, Bobby Burns.
Chartreuse	herbs and spices	Alaska.
Cherry Brandy	cherry	Singapore Sling.
Coconut liqueur	coconut	Coconut Daiquiri, Pink Grapefruit.
Cointreau	orange	Balalaika, Between-the-Sheets, Fluffy Duck, Golden Dream, Maiden's Prayer, Margarita,

Liqueur	Flavour	Recipes
Cointreau (cont.)	orange	Rolls Royce, Scotch Frog, Sidecar, Silent Third, Velvet Hammer, White Lady, X.Y.Z., Yellow Bird.
Crème de Banane	banana	Banana Daiquiri.
Crème de Cacao	chocolate	Alexander, Barbara, Fifth Avenue, Frozen Alexander, Golden Cadillac, Grasshopper, Russian Cocktail, Silk Stockings.
Crème de Cassis	blackcurrant	Cardinale, Kir, Kir Royale, Vermouth Cassis.
Crème de Menthe	peppermint	Chocolate Mint Fizz, Fernet Menthe, Grasshopper, Snapdragon, Stinger, White Spider.
Curaçao	orange	Bleu-Do-It, Blue Lagoon, Blue Hawaiian, Bosom Caresser, Brandy Crusta, Mai Tai, Margarita, Rhett Butler.

Liqueur	Flavour	Recipes
Drambuie	honey and whisky	Golden Glow, Rusty Nail, Scotch Milk.
Galliano	liquorice	Freddie Fudpucker, Gold Cup, Golden Cadillac, Golden Dream, Golden Glow, Golden Medallion, Harvey Wallbanger, Italian Heather, Scotch Frog, Yellow Bird.
Irish Mist	herbs and whiskey	Ginger Mist, Strawberry Blonde.
Kahlua	coffee	Black Russian, Brave Bull, White Russian
Kummel	caraway seeds	Glass Slipper, Silver Bullet, Silver Streak.
Mandarine Napoléon	tangerine	Appetizer, Brewer Street Rascal, Frozen Mandarine Sour, Mandarine Sour, Tidal Wave, Tropical Tonic, Waterloo.
Maraschino	cherry	Brandy Crusta, Frozen Daiquiri.

Liqueur	Flavour	Recipes
Midori	musk melon	Emerald Sparkler, Frozen Melon Sour, Kicker, Melon Daiquiri, Tokyo Joe.
Nassau Orange	bitter orange	Nassau Express.
Pastis	liquorice	Macaroni, Sazerac, Suissesse, Tiger's Tail.
Royal Mint Chocolate	peppermint and chocolate	After Eight, Mint Royal.
Southern Comfort	peach	Rhett Butler, Sicilian Kiss.
Tia Maria	coffee	Easter Egg, Velvet Hammer.

Party Drinks

There is an art to giving a successful party and no matter how many guests are expected, the formula is always the same. Thorough preparation is absolutely essential so that when guests arrive the host and hostess are calm, properly dressed and obviously looking forward to their company.

Conversation comes easily in an atmosphere of relaxation, and within a short while there is a happy buzz in the air. It is difficult for guests to feel at ease if the hostess only appears when food is served and disappears immediately afterwards or the host can be heard frantically smashing away at blocks of ice. Attention to detail before the party ensures that everything remains under control throughout the evening. This is the very simple secret of entertaining.

Several Days Before the Party

Plan a food menu. For the majority of cocktail parties it is sufficient to serve finger food. This is a phrase open to interpretation, but aim to provide nibbles that can be prepared well in advance and served with maximum presentation and a minimum of fuss. Spare a thought for the guest who has to eat standing up, usually with a glass in one hand. Food that requires a plate and fork is all very well with small numbers, but if the gathering is quite large, choose food that can be passed around and offer large absorbent napkins.

Prepare a comprehensive shopping list and buy all non-perishables including liquor and minerals.

Polish glassware and cutlery. It is a good idea to

allocate a bench or cabinet top as the assembly point for all containers such as bowls, baskets, vases and dishes that will be needed, so avoiding a last-minute scramble to find a particular item. On the day this 'collection' serves as a valuable checking system because each container on the bench top signals a job still to be completed.

The Day Before the Party
Buy in the perishable food, fruit, fruit juices and flowers.

Clean the house and arrange the flowers.

Carry out as much of the food preparation as possible.

Check that there is an adequate supply of ice ready for the following day.

The Day of the Party
Crush as much ice as will be needed for all the evening's drinks, dry it on a cloth, put into a sizeable container and replace in the freezer. This way it will stay dry and hard allowing it to last longer at room temperature.

Set up the bar area so that it is easily accessible.

Prepare all the garnishes. It does not matter if too much is prepared as it is better to waste an orange or lemon than to interrupt the flow of drinks by spending time searching for a cutting board, knife and more fruit which will probably end up in larger-than-life-sized slices because of haste.

Set up a large disposal bag so that it is permanently open. This way waste can be quickly and easily dispensed with while the party is in progress.

Allocate a section of the kitchen bench space to food preparation and another to drink preparation. This avoids the needless aggravation that arises when the host is blending Pina Coladas while the hostess is trying to whip the cream.

Any extra supplies that *might* be needed during the evening should be stacked in an easily accessible spot.

Once everything is ready, the sink must be left completely clear for safety's sake as well as ease of operation later in the evening.

Make sure there are plenty of ash-trays available.

Finish all preparation in time to have a hot bath or a relaxing drink, so that guests arrive to a warm welcome and happy household.

CHOOSING THE DRINKS

The most suitable cocktails for a party are those which look attractive and inviting to drink and can be mixed easily and quickly. Cocktails can be very little trouble to serve to a large number of people as long as the preparation is done thoroughly.

When choosing, consider the capacity of the kitchen to cope with behind-the-scenes groundwork, the availability of enough correct glassware and the length of time it takes to prepare each drink.

The host or hostess should decide which cocktails are to be served as most guests are happy to choose from three or four different suggestions. It can be fun to write the names of the chosen cocktails on a blackboard or wall poster as this adds to the atmosphere and saves much explanation. Also, when choosing the drinks for a party, ensure

that at least one of them is non-alcoholic. Ask one other person to help dispense drinks so that the bar area is manned at all times. It is best if guests do not have to pour their own as this can cause stock problems and also increases the risk of accidents.

Drinks such as the Bloody Mary, Sangria and Punches, which can be prepared in quantity and transferred to jugs, benefit from being made a couple of hours in advance. The Harvey Wall-banger, Tiger's Tail and Freddie Fudpucker can also be prepared in quantity and only need to be well stirred before being poured into ice-filled glasses. Drinks requiring topping up or mixing with carbonated minerals such as tonic and soda water can be made up beforehand, providing the mineral is added just prior to service.

GLASSWARE

Simple procedures will make it easier to maintain the same standard of drink and service all evening and allow the host to relax as well. The cost of hiring a few dozen glasses is minimal and it is a positive advantage to have quite a number of them as it is faster to collect dirty glasses and recycle them, so that each drink is served in a fresh one, than to spend time matching each guest to his glass. Restrict glassware to two shapes, preferably the highball which suits all long drinks and the all-purpose Paris goblet. A tray of drinks offered around at regular intervals ensures that conversations do not have to be interrupted while one member of the group wanders off to replenish glasses.

Bellini
1 part peach juice
3 parts chilled champagne
Serve in a tulip or flute glass.

Brewer Street Rascal
1 part vodka
1 part Mandarine Napoléon
4 parts grapefruit juice
1 dash egg white
Shake. Serve in a wine goblet. Decorate with a wedge of grapefruit or a slice of orange.

Buck's Fizz
1 part orange juice
3 parts chilled champagne
Serve in a tulip or flute glass.

Cool Shower
1 part Campari
2 parts orange juice
3 parts dry sparkling wine
rind of orange
Put the rind from an orange and some ice cubes in a goblet. Add the Campari, the orange juice and the dry sparkling wine.

Country Club Cooler
1 part dry vermouth
2 parts ginger ale
2 dashes grenadine
Mix together in a tall tumbler. Add a spiral of lemon and a spiral of orange to dangle over the edge of the glass. Anchor with ice cubes.

Cuba Libre
1 part white rum
4 parts cola
juice of $\frac{1}{2}$ fresh lime
Mix together in an ice-filled highball glass. Drop in the spent shell of the lime. Serve with straws.

Emerald Sparkler

1 part Midori
3 parts dry sparkling wine
Serve in a champagne flute glass.

Freddie Fudpucker

1 part tequila
4 parts orange juice
1 dash Galliano
Stir the tequila and the orange juice into an ice-filled highball glass. Float a dash of Galliano on the top. Serve with straws.

Ginger Mist

1 part Irish Mist
5 parts dry ginger ale
1 lemon wedge
Stir the Irish Mist and the ginger ale into an ice-filled highball glass. Squeeze a wedge of lemon over the top.

Harvey Wallbanger

1 part vodka
3 parts orange juice
2 dashes Galliano
Mix vodka and orange juice together in an ice-filled tall glass. Splash in 2 dashes of Galliano.

Horse's Neck

1 part brandy
4 parts ginger ale
1 dash Angostura bitters
Mix together in an ice-filled highball glass. Add a spiral of lemon.

Kir Royale

2 dashes crème de cassis
chilled champagne
Put 2 dashes of crème de cassis into a tulip or flute glass. Top up with chilled champagne.

Machete
1 part vodka
2 parts pineapple juice
3 parts tonic
Mix in an ice-filled highball glass.

Moscow Mule
2 parts vodka
juice of 1 lime
4 parts ginger beer
Mix together in an ice-filled highball glass. Drop in the spent shell of the lime.

Pigs in Space
1 part golden rum
2 dashes Angostura bitters
5 parts dry ginger ale
Stir the rum and Angostura bitters into a highball glass which contains some ice. Add the 5 parts of ginger ale and add a twist of orange peel.

Salty Dog
1 part vodka
4 parts grapefruit juice
Salt the rim of a large goblet and fill with ice. Add the vodka and the grapefruit juice.

Screwdriver
1 part vodka
4 parts orange juice
Mix together in a large ice-filled glass.

Snapdragon
2 parts vodka
1 part crème de menthe
3 parts soda water
Stir the vodka and crème de menthe into an ice-filled highball glass. Top with the soda water.

Stone Fence

1 part Scotch or bourbon whisky
4 parts dry cider

Mix together in an ice-filled highball glass. Add a twist of lemon peel.

Strawberry Blonde

1 part Irish Mist
2 strawberries
1 scoop crushed ice
2 parts dry sparkling wine

Blend the Irish Mist, the strawberries and the crushed ice and pour into a flute glass. Top with dry sparkling wine.

Tidal Wave

1 part Mandarine Napoléon
4 parts bitter lemon
1 dash lemon juice

Mix together in an ice-filled highball glass. Add a slice of lemon.

Tiger's Tail

1 part pastis
2 parts orange juice

Mix together in an ice-filled old-fashioned glass. Add a slice of orange.

Tropical Tonic

2 parts Malibu
1 part Mandarine Napoléon
5 parts dry ginger ale

Stir the Malibu and the Mandarine Napoléon together in an ice-filled highball glass. Top with dry ginger ale.

Waterloo

1 part Mandarine Napoléon
4 parts orange juice

Mix together in an ice-filled highball glass.

Summer Drinks

Warm weather and long cool drinks go together. There is nothing like the sight of a tall frosted glass brimming with refreshment to lift morale on a hot day. The essence of a cooling drink is that it has a fairly low alcohol content, has plenty of flavour and is served in large quantity. For this reason the highball glass which holds 8–12 oz/ 225–350 ml is ideal for long drinks.

Some of the more famous recipes in the cocktail world are long drinks that were first mixed in hot climates. The Mint Julep has been lovingly prepared in the Southern States of the U.S.A. for generations, and Southerners still enjoy the continuing debate as to whether the mint should be crushed or not. Whichever way it is preferred, every visitor to the Kentucky Derby samples a Mint Julep or two as the drink has become a part of the race day.

The British took their love of gin with them to the colonies during the reign of Queen Victoria. It was in the Far East that gin and tonic became inseparable. A good measure of gin with plenty of ice, tonic and a slice of lemon or lime squeezed into the glass is one of the most thirst quenching of all drinks. This drink had an added advantage as the quinine content of the tonic was an active ingredient in the fight against malaria.

Many long drinks have a rum base, because rum is distilled from sugar cane, which grows profusely in tropical climates. The Planter's Punch is widely consumed in the Caribbean and the Scorpion is a

favourite throughout Polynesia.

, Now that the electric blender is widely available, there are many new long drinks becoming popular, the most well known being the Pina Colada. Coconut cream blended with other ingredients gives a mousse-like texture, and drinks that are blended with plenty of crushed ice take on a sorbet (U.S. sherbet) texture which is particularly refreshing. Ice-cream is a relatively new ingredient in cocktails and it makes delicious creamy drinks which are often appreciated after dinner as well as on hot days. There are numerous combinations of spirits, liqueurs, creams and juices suitable for the blender and experimenting with blended drinks is fun.

Banana Daiquiri
2 parts white rum
1 part fresh lime juice
2 dashes crème de banane
$\frac{1}{2}$ banana
2 scoops crushed ice
Blend. Serve in a goblet with straws.

Blue Hawaiian

2 parts white rum
1 part blue curaçao
4 parts pineapple juice
1 part coconut cream
1 scoop crushed ice

Blend and then pour into a large-bowled glass.

Bulldog Cooler

1 large measure gin
2 dashes lemon juice
2 dashes gomme syrup
ginger ale

Mix the gin, the lemon juice and the gomme syrup together in a highball glass. Top with ginger ale. Decorate with a spiral of lemon.

Chi Chi

2 parts vodka
1 part coconut cream
4 parts pineapple juice
2 scoops crushed ice

Blend and then pour into a large-bowled glass. Decorate with a slice of pineapple and a cherry.

Collins – John or Tom

1 part gin
1 part lemon juice
2 dashes gomme syrup
soda water

Mix gin, lemon juice, and syrup together in an ice-filled highball glass. Top up with soda. Add a slice of lemon and serve with straws.

Fluffy Duck

3 parts gin
3 parts advocaat
2 parts orange juice
2 parts Cointreau
6 parts soda water

Mix gin, advocaat, orange juice and Cointreau together in an ice-filled highball glass. Top with 6 parts of soda. Serve with straws.

Frozen Daiquiri
2 parts white rum
1 part fresh lime juice
1 dash maraschino
1 dash gomme syrup
2 scoops crushed ice

Blend and then pour into a goblet. Serve with straws.

Gin Sling
2 parts gin
1 part lemon juice
3 parts soda water

Mix together in an ice-filled highball glass.

Limbo
1 part peach brandy
4 parts pineapple juice

Serve over ice in a highball glass.

Melon Daiquiri
2 parts white rum
1 part fresh lime juice
2 dashes Midori liqueur
2 scoops crushed ice

Blend. Serve in a goblet with straws.

Mint Julep
6–8 leaves fresh mint
1 tablespoon sugar
1 tablespoon water
1 measure bourbon

Place 4–5 leaves of mint in a highball glass. Sprinkle sugar and water over the leaves and crush together until the sugar is dissolved and the flavour extracted from the mint. Add bourbon and crushed ice and stir until the glass is frosted. Decorate with mint and serve with straws.

Pina Colada
2 parts white rum
2 parts pineapple juice
1 part coconut cream
2 scoops crushed ice
Blend. Serve in a large-bowled glass. Decorate with chunks of pineapple and a cherry. Serve with straws.

Pink Grapefruit
1 part Malibu
2 parts grapefruit juice
1 dash Campari
Stir the Malibu and the grapefruit juice in a goblet. Splash with a dash of Campari and decorate with a red cherry.

Planter's Punch
1 part dark rum
1 part lemon juice
1 dash Angostura bitters
3 dashes grenadine
soda water
Mix rum, lemon juice, bitters and grenadine together in an ice-filled highball glass. Top with soda water and decorate with a slice of lemon and a slice of orange.

Quiet Sunday
1 part vodka
4 parts orange juice
3 dashes amaretto
few drops grenadine
Shake vodka, orange juice and amaretto and pour into an ice-filled highball glass. Add a few drops of grenadine.

Rhett Butler

2 parts Southern Comfort
2 parts orange curaçao
1 part lime juice
1 part lemon juice
4 parts soda water

Shake Southern Comfort, orange curacao, lime juice and lemon juice and strain into an ice-filled highball glass. Top with soda water and decorate with a slice of orange and a sprig of mint.

Scorpion

3 parts golden rum
2 parts orange juice
2 parts lemon juice
1 part brandy
2 dashes orgeat syrup
1 scoop crushed ice

Blend. Serve in an old-fashioned glass. Decorate with a slice of orange and some leaves of mint.

Singapore Sling

2 parts gin
1 part cherry brandy
1 part lemon juice
soda water

Shake the gin, cherry brandy, and lemon juice together and strain into an ice-filled highball glass. Top with soda water and add a slice of orange.

Strawberry Daiquiri

2 parts white rum
1 part fresh lime juice
2 dashes fraise liqueur
3 fresh strawberries
2 scoops of crushed ice

Blend and then pour into a goblet. Serve with straws.

Strawberry Dawn
1 part gin
1 part coconut cream
2–3 fresh strawberries
2 scoops crushed ice
Blend. Serve in a large-bowled glass. Decorate with a strawberry and serve with straws.

Tequila Sunrise
1 part tequila
4 parts orange juice
1 dash grenadine
Stir the tequila and orange juice together in an ice-filled highball glass. Splash a little grenadine on top. Add a slice of orange and a cherry and serve with straws.

ICE CREAM DRINKS
Chocolate-Mint-Fizz
1 part white rum
6 parts chocolate ice-cream
2 dashes green crème de menthe
Blend. Serve in a goblet and supply short straws.

Easter Egg
1 part advocaat
1 part Tia Maria
2 scoops chocolate ice-cream
Blend.

Frozen Alexander
1 part brandy
1 part brown crème de cacao
1 scoop vanilla ice-cream
Blend.

Frozen Apricot Sour
2 parts apricot brandy
1 part lemon juice
1 scoop vanilla ice-cream
Blend. Serve in a wine goblet.

Frozen Mandarine Sour

2 parts Mandarine Napoléon
1 part lemon juice
1 scoop vanilla ice-cream
Blend. Serve in a wine goblet.

Frozen Melon Sour

2 parts Midori liqueur
1 part lemon juice
1 scoop vanilla ice-cream
Blend. Serve in a wine goblet.

Glass Slipper

2 parts vodka
1 part kummel
1 scoop vanilla ice-cream
Blend. Serve in a champagne saucer with two short straws.

Nassau Express

2 parts Nassau Orange liqueur
1 part brandy
2 scoops coffee ice-cream
a few ice cubes
Blend. Strain into a cocktail glass and then dust top with instant coffee.

Wintery Warmers

In cold weather, thoughts turn naturally to hot drinks. Skiers return to their chalets for a fortifying tankard of mulled wine, the Germans are fond of their Glühwein and many an Englishman has been known to retire to the fireside with his hot toddy.

Sailors have long found a good tot of rum to be an effective weapon against the inhospitable weather often experienced at sea and until recently, the British Navy issued every sailor with a daily ration of rum for precisely this reason. In fact one Admiral, nicknamed 'Old Grog', thought his crew took to the rum ration a little too enthusiastically so he had it watered down, thus earning himself everlasting recognition: any spirit drink, topped up with hot water, is now known as Grog.

Hot drinks are particularly welcome at Christmas time and in many parts of the world it is traditional to offer guests a glass of hot punch or mulled red wine as soon as they arrive. The aroma of the steamy liquid revives flagging spirits and the hot bracing flavour warms right through to the toes.

When preparing hot drinks, it is important to select the right glassware. Make sure the glass is strong enough to stand the heat and put a metal spoon into the glass before pouring in the liquid, so that excess heat passes into the spoon rather than the glass. Choose a style of glassware with a handle or stem so that the glass can be handled while the drink is still hot. Do not overheat the drink as this will drive off the alcohol content and use restraint when preparing a hot drink with a spirit base because too much alcohol gives off a very heady aroma and makes it difficult to imbibe until it has cooled down.

SPECIALITY COFFEES

Hot coffee, laced with spirit and topped with cream, makes an excellent finish to a dinner party. It is also a very relaxing drink to have late at night. The most famous combination of spirit and coffee is known as Irish Coffee and there are a few simple steps to making this delicious concoction.

Irish Coffee

3 coffee spoons demerara or light brown sugar
hot black coffee
1 measure Irish whiskey
fresh cream

Put the sugar into a heat-resistant glass and $\frac{3}{4}$ fill with hot black coffee. Stir until the sugar is dissolved. Add the Irish whiskey and stir. Pour the cream over the back of a teaspoon and it will float on top of the coffee. Serve with a napkin. The coffee is sipped through the cream.

These are the most popular of the other combinations of spirit, hot coffee and cream:

Calypso coffee	—	Tia Maria
Caribbean coffee	—	rum
Coffee Royale	—	cognac
Gaelic coffee	—	Scotch whisky
German coffee	—	kirsch
Italian coffee	—	Strega
Monks coffee	—	Benedictine
Normandy coffee	—	calvados
Prince Charles coffee	—	Drambuie
Roman coffee	—	Galliano
Scandinavian coffee	—	akvavit

Glühwein
½ pint/300 ml red wine
2 sugar cubes
2 cloves
1 cinnamon stick
1 slice of lemon
Boil all the ingredients together and serve in a heat-resistant glass.

Gold Cup
4 cups weak tea
¼ cup sugar
5 cups orange juice
¾ cup Galliano
1 cinnamon stick
Heat gently. Garnish with fresh mint and orange slices.

Grog
1 part Jamaican rum
4 parts boiling water
juice of ½ lemon
1 sugar cube
a few cloves
1 cinnamon stick
Combine all the ingredients but the boiling water in a mug. Add boiling water until the sugar dissolves.

Hot Brown Cow
3 parts hot milk
3 parts hot black coffee
2 parts dark rum
Stir together in a heat-resistant glass.

Hot Buttered Rum
1 measure dark rum
1 sugar cube
1 slice butter
4 cloves

Mix all the ingredients together in a heat-resistant old-fashioned glass. Fill with boiling water.

Hot Scotch Toddy
4 parts Scotch whisky
1 part fresh lemon juice
3 dashes Angostura bitters
2 dashes gomme syrup or honey
5 parts boiling water
Mix together in a tankard. Serve with a napkin.

Hot Shot
1 part vodka
4 parts beef consommé
1 dash lemon juice
2 dashes Worcestershire sauce
1 pinch celery salt
Heat the ingredients gently and pour into an old-fashioned glass.

Hot Toddy
1 measure desired spirit
3 dashes gomme syrup
Mix spirit and gomme syrup in a heat-resistant glass. Top up with boiling water. Add a slice of lemon and sprinkle nutmeg on top.

Icebreaker
1 part dark rum
1 teaspoon sugar
1 pinch ground cinnamon
4 parts hot weak tea
Stir the rum, sugar and cinnamon together in a mug. Top with hot weak tea.

Liqueur Punch
1 dash ginger wine
1 dash liqueur
3 cloves
hot tea
1 pinch ground cinnamon
1 pinch nutmeg

Place cloves in a stemmed glass. Fill with hot tea. Add a dash of ginger wine, a pinch of cinnamon and a pinch of nutmeg. Top with a dash of any liqueur.

Nightcap
1 part dark rum
1 teaspoon sugar
warm milk

Mix dark rum and sugar together in an old-fashioned glass and top with warm milk. Dust the top with nutmeg.

Scotch Milk
2 parts Scotch whisky
1 part Drambuie
1 teaspoon finely granulated white sugar
1 pinch ground cinnamon
5 parts hot milk

Stir all the ingredients together in a mug.

Whisky Mac
2 parts Scotch whisky
1 part ginger wine

Serve straight into an old-fashioned glass.

Drinks for Dieters

Weight watching has become one of today's most absorbing pastimes. Almost everyone has suffered the pangs of guilt that accompany the letting out of a couple of notches on a belt. When that favourite outfit causes physical discomfort, the time has come to review eating and drinking habits.

Numerous diet plans are readily available and most people can follow one of them quite happily. Also, the problem of how to stick to a diet and still maintain a normal social life without being dubbed the biggest bore in town can be solved by following a few basic rules.

Make up your mind before you go out whether you are going to drink alcohol at all on that particular occasion. If not, then decide on a couple of non-alcoholic drinks that you prefer and, when asked what you wish to drink, order one of them as naturally as you would a gin and tonic. Do not fuss or hesitate about it and the company will accept your choice in the same manner. If you are pressured, smile politely and stick by your original decision. In many situations it will attract less comment to have a Pussyfoot or Virgin Mary than to order just a cola or orange juice.

Cocktails that are lightly alcoholic are a blessing to the weight watcher. Many of today's popular cocktails are long drinks with lots of ice and fruit juices. They can be sipped slowly and have the added advantage of tasting delicious. Drinks topped up with soda water are also suitable and slimline minerals should be ordered wherever possible.

Wine contains some carbohydrates but spirits do not, and beer has a very high carbohydrate count. For those who count calories, the approximate numbers per oz/25 ml for alcoholic drinks are: dry wine 20, sweet wine 25, dry sherry 33, spirits 63, dry vermouth 27, sweet vermouth 44, liqueurs 90, beer 10. However, remember that a 6-oz/175-ml glass of wine or a half pint/300 ml of lager has a much higher calorie count than a Spritzer or a brandy and soda.

It is best to establish a sensible drinking pattern that suits your way of life, then abide by it until it becomes a habit.

Almond Fizz
2 parts orgeat syrup
1 part lime juice
soda water
Shake orgeat syrup and lime juice together with ice cubes and strain into an ice-filled highball glass. Top up with soda and serve with straws.

Banana Whip
4 oz/100 ml cold milk
1 small egg
1 ripe banana
½ teaspoon nutmeg
Blend. Serve in a highball glass.

Clementine

1 part orange juice
1 part Perrier water

Mix together in an ice-filled highball glass. Add a slice of orange.

Coconut Palm

3 parts pineapple juice
1 part grapefruit juice
1 part coconut cream
2 scoops crushed ice

Blend. Pour into a highball glass and serve with straws.

Pussyfoot

1 part orange juice
1 part lemon juice
1 part lime juice
1 dash grenadine
1 egg yolk

Shake.

Sangria

1 bottle red wine
$\frac{1}{4}$ cup sugar
1 cup water
1 orange (thinly sliced)
1 lime (thinly sliced)
1 lemon (thinly sliced)
6 oz/175 ml soda water

Dissolve the sugar in the water. Place all the ingredients, except the soda water, in a jug and refrigerate for at least an hour. When ready to serve, add some ice cubes and the soda water.
Makes 6 glasses

Shirley Temple

ginger ale
grenadine

Top an ice-filled highball glass with ginger ale. Add a little grenadine and stir gently. Decorate with cherries.

Snowball
1 oz/25 ml advocaat
1 dash lime juice
carbonated lemonade or 7-Up
Put the advocaat and lime juice into an ice-filled
highball glass. Top up with lemonade and
decorate with a slice of orange and a cherry.

Spritzer
1 part dry white wine
1 part soda water
Mix together in an ice-filled goblet. Add a twist of
lemon.

Vermouth Cassis
2 parts dry vermouth
1 part crème de cassis
2 parts soda
Stir the dry vermouth and the crème de cassis
together with ice in a highball glass. Top with
soda water.

Virgin Mary
4 oz/100 ml tomato juice
1 dash lemon juice
2 dashes Worcestershire sauce
2 pinches celery salt
Shake. Strain into an ice-filled highball glass.

For the Morning After

Most imbibers have suffered at some time from the after-effect of a particularly enthusiastic encounter with alcohol. Hangovers usually manifest themselves as a complete loss of any desire to move the head for fear of the hammering pain or the sufferer's stomach takes on a life of its own and completely dominates all thoughts for the rest of the morning as the owner struggles valiantly to regain control of it. Some particularly unfortunate individuals are inflicted with both these problems at once. It would seem, too, that the hangover recognizes no nationality as the German word for it is '*katzenjammer*' which translates as 'wailing of cats'.

A hangover is really the body's message that it is in an advanced state of dehydration as too much alcohol affects that part of the brain which regulates fluid elimination. Once this has happened, only water and time are of any real assistance. Carbon dioxide accelerates the rate of absorption from the stomach into the blood stream which is why effervescent substances such

as seltzers and soda water are popular cures.

It is best to take as much precaution as possible to avoid dehydration, not only because of its painful side effects but because it does real damage to the body. Water is the vital fluid that allows the body's organs to function efficiently and lack of it is dangerous to health. It is most helpful to eat before drinking as food absorbs some of the alcohol, so slowing down its passage into the bloodstream. Meat, eggs and other high-protein foods are particularly effective foods and, at the very least, a large glass of milk will line the stomach and act as an insulator to some degree.

The comparison between alcohol and electricity is an apt one as they are both very good friends but deadly enemies. The host or hostess has a responsibility to serve alcohol sensibly so that guests enjoy themselves fully without developing into crashing bores or sleeping beauties. Also, it must be remembered in this modern age that 'breathalyzer' is *not* the name of a cocktail!

Bloody Mary
1 part vodka
4 parts tomato juice
1 dash lemon juice
2 dashes Worcestershire sauce
1 pinch celery salt
Tabasco sauce
pepper

Mix vodka, tomato juice, lemon juice, Worcestershire sauce and celery salt together. Put into a tall glass with ice or serve chilled in a goblet. Add Tabasco sauce and pepper to taste.

Corpse-Reviver
2 parts brandy
1 part calvados
1 part sweet vermouth

Serve chilled. Add a twist of lemon.

Danish Mary

1 part akvavit
4 parts tomato juice
1 dash lemon juice
2 dashes Worcestershire sauce
1 pinch celery salt

Mix together in an ice-filled highball glass.

Egg Nog

1 part brandy
1 part dark rum
1 egg
2 dashes gomme syrup
3 parts milk

Shake brandy, rum, egg and syrup together and strain into a large goblet. Add the milk. Grate some nutmeg on top.

Fernet Menthe

2 parts Fernet Branca
1 part green crème de menthe

Serve chilled.

Hair of the Dog

1 part Scotch whisky
2 parts cream
1 part honey

Shake. Strain into a cocktail glass.

Prairie Oyster

1 unbroken egg yolk
1 dash ketchup
2 dashes vinegar
1 dash pepper

Put the ingredients into a small wine glass and drink in one swallow.

81

Potent Concoctions

Drinks created at home are frequently very alcoholic as the home bartender can be over-enthusiastic when mixing recipes. However, it is fun to create new cocktail recipes and to try them out as 'house specialities' on guests. Remember that the most successful drinks are those which abide by the well-tried formula of including a base, a modifier and perhaps a touch of something special.

There are a number of famous cocktails that are quite potent, but because they obey the rules of 'mixology', they are well-balanced, flavoursome drinks. In most of these recipes the alcohol content is used to define the flavour constituents of the ingredients in much the same manner as red ink is used to underline something important in a document.

Most spirits are about 40% alcohol by volume and the law requires that the alcoholic content be stated on the label. Liqueurs vary from 17% to 54% alcohol by volume. Crème de cassis, other crème liqueurs, apricot and cherry brandies are towards the lower end of the alcoholic scale while beverages such as Cointreau, Drambuie, Galliano and Pernod have the same alcoholic content as spirits. Table wines contain between 7% and 14% alcohol depending on their country or origin: white wine from Germany can be 9% and a Spanish white wine can be over 12%. Sherry, port and Madeira are fortified wines, which means that brandy has been added to them, and they are about 20% alcohol. Vermouths are approximately 17% alcohol by volume, and beers range from around 4% for ale to 10% for some strong beers.

Perhaps the most well known of potent long drinks is the Zombie which contains four different rums and a liqueur. It is interesting to note that the Zombie has created a worldwide demand for 151-proof Demeraran rum which is 86% alcohol. Prior to the invention of the Zombie this particular strength of rum was consumed mainly by lumberjacks in Alaska.

Alaska
3 parts gin
1 part yellow Chartreuse
Shake.

Bleu-Do-It
1 part gin
1 part vodka
1 part tequila
1 part blue curaçao
2 parts lemon juice
1 dash egg white
2 parts soda water
Shake all the ingredients but the soda water and strain into an ice-filled highball glass. Top up with the soda.

Brandy Cocktail
4 parts brandy
1 part sweet vermouth
1 dash Angostura bitters
Serve chilled. Add a cherry.

Bunny Hug
1 part gin
1 part whisky
1 part Pernod
Shake.

French Connection
1 part brandy
1 part amaretto
Serve over ice in an old-fashioned glass.

Gibson
6 parts gin
1 part dry vermouth
Serve chilled or on the rocks. Add a pearl onion for decoration.

Godfather
2 parts Scotch whisky or bourbon
1 part amaretto
Serve over ice in an old-fashioned glass.

Godmother
2 parts vodka
1 part amaretto
Serve over ice in an old-fashioned glass.

Iceberg
1 large measure vodka
1 dash Pernod
Pour vodka over ice in an old-fashioned glass and add a dash of Pernod.

Italian Heather
4 parts Scotch whisky
1 part Galliano
Stir ingredients into a glass with ice. Serve with a twist of lemon.

Kicker
1 part whisky
1 part Midori liqueur
Serve chilled or on the rocks.

Mai Tai

2 parts white rum
2 parts golden rum
1 part orange curaçao
2 dashes orgeat syrup
1 dash grenadine
juice of 1 lime

Mix together in a large old-fashioned glass. Decorate with mint, pineapple and the spent shell of the lime.

Margarita

2 parts tequila
2 parts fresh lime juice
1 part Cointreau
lemon
salt

Rub the rim of the cocktail glass with lemon to moisten, then dip it in salt. Shake the remaining ingredients together and pour into prepared glass.

Old-Fashioned

1 sugar cube
3 dashes Angostura bitters
1 large measure rye whisky

Put the sugar and the bitters into an old-fashioned glass and add enough water to dissolve the sugar (about a spoonful). Fill with ice and add a large measure of rye whisky. Add a slice of orange and a cherry.

Russian Cocktail
1 part vodka
1 part gin
1 part brown crème de cacao
Shake.

Rusty Nail
2 parts Scotch whisky
1 part Drambuie
Mix together in an ice-filled old-fashioned glass.
Add a twist of lemon peel.

Scotch Mist
1 large measure Scotch whisky
Shake the whisky together with crushed ice and
pour, unstrained, into an old-fashioned glass.
Add a twist of lemon.

Sicilian Kiss
1 part amaretto
1 part Southern Comfort
Serve chilled.

Silver Bullet
2 parts vodka
1 part kummel
Serve chilled or on the rocks.

Silver Streak
2 parts gin
1 part kummel
Serve chilled or on the rocks.

Stinger
2 parts brandy
1 part white crème de menthe
Serve chilled or on the rocks.

Tokyo Joe
1 part vodka
1 part Midori liqueur
Serve chilled or on the rocks.

White Spider
2 parts vodka
1 part white crème de menthe
Serve chilled or on the rocks.

Zombie
2 parts white rum
2 parts golden rum
2 parts dark rum
1 part apricot brandy
1 part lime juice
1 part pineapple juice
1 dash gomme syrup
1 splash Demeraran rum

Shake the white rum, golden rum, dark rum, apricot brandy, lime juice, pineapple juice and gomme syrup and serve in an ice-filled highball glass. Splash in 151 proof Demeraran rum. Decorate with a sprig of fresh mint.

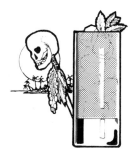

Classic Cocktail Styles

Cobbler A long drink, usually of wine, port or sherry, sweetened with a liqueur and served over ice.

Collins A long drink of gin, lemon, sugar, ice and soda water. Originally a Tom Collins was made with 'Old Tom Gin' which is sweeter than other gins.

Cooler This long icy drink is very similar to a collins but often contains a long spiral of fruit rind.

Crusta A medium-sized drink served in a frosted sugar-rimmed goblet and made with a spirit, fruit juice and liqueurs. The best known is the Brandy Crusta.

Cups Concoctions of wine, liqueurs and fruit juices. They are served well-iced and are often made in large quantities, suitable for parties.

Daiquiri The daiquiri is a short drink with white rum, lime juice and sugar syrup. This refreshing combination adapts well to the blender and frozen daiquiris are made by adding fresh fruit and plenty of crushed ice to the basic ingredients. After blending frozen daiquiris have the texture of a sorbet (U.S. sherbet) and are served in a long glass with straws.

Egg Nog Egg nogs are based on egg and milk with a spirit added. They are regarded as morning 'reviver' drinks and may be made in large quantities.

Fizz A fizz is, traditionally, a shaken drink served in a tall glass. It separates quickly and so must be drunk immediately. A number of champagne-based drinks are sometimes referred to as fizzes.

Flip A flip is an egg, sugar and liquor drink that is shaken and strained into a small glass. It is sometimes regarded as a pick-me-up or a bed-time drink.

Frappé One or more liqueurs are poured over finely crushed ice in a long-stemmed glass and sipped through a short straw. This very refreshing drink is often served after dinner. A spirit shaken with crushed ice and poured unstrained is called a mist.

Highball This classic American iced long drink is simply made by topping up a measure of

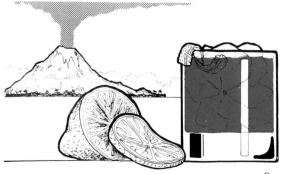

spirit with a mineral or soda water. Well known highballs are the Rye Highball, Cuba Libre and Horse's Neck.

Julep The essential ingredient of a Julep is fresh mint which is crushed in a glass with sugar. Spirit and ice are added and it is served in a frosted glass. This is the drink most popular in the 'Deep South' in the U.S.A.

Punch Originally punch had a rum base and contained other spirits and fruit juices. Today it can contain a varied combination of ingredients. It is easily mixed in large quantities and can be served hot or cold.

Sling The sling is a close cousin of the collins, as it is a long iced drink. The Gin Sling was the favourite drink of army officers during the days of the British Empire and is thought to have been concocted in the Far East. The most well-known is the Singapore Sling.

Sour This is a tangy combination of spirit or liqueur, citrus juice, sugar and egg white. Its sharpness makes it an excellent before-dinner cocktail. It is essential that the lemon juice be freshly squeezed. The most popular of these drinks is the Whisky Sour.

Toddy A toddy contains spirit, sugar, water and spices. In the reign of Queen Victoria, a lady would take a hot toddy to calm her nerves but today it may be served hot or cold.

Index

91